LAKE CONSTANCE TRAVEL GUIDE

SECRETS OF THE LAKE: NATURE, HISTORY, AND ADVENTURE AWAIT

Sam Oxford

TABLE OF CONTENTS

CHAPTER 1

INTRODUCTION TO LAKE CONSTANCE

Nestled at the intersection of Germany, Austria, and Switzerland, Lake Constance is a breathtaking gem in Central Europe, inviting travelers to lose themselves in a landscape where mountains meet water and cultures intertwine. Known locally as "Bodensee," this 63-kilometer-long lake is not only one of Europe's largest but also a vibrant and captivating destination that brings together historical charm, natural beauty, and a rich tapestry of traditions and experiences. Whether you're a history enthusiast, a nature lover, or simply someone seeking a place to unwind, Lake Constance has something for everyone.

Stretching along the Rhine River, Lake Constance has played an important role throughout European history. Once a central point for trade and diplomacy, the lake has seen Roman settlements, medieval fortresses, and vibrant towns spring up along its shores, each leaving behind remnants of a time long gone yet profoundly alive in the architecture, culture, and traditions that remain today. Today, the lake is divided into two main sections: the larger Upper Lake (Obersee) and the more intimate Lower Lake (Untersee), both connected by the Rhine, which flows from its source in the Swiss Alps, through Lake Constance, and onward to the North Sea.

The region's surrounding landscape is equally remarkable. To the east, you'll find views of the Alps, which stand like silent guardians over the lake, while lush rolling vineyards and orchards cascade down toward the shoreline. These settings have inspired countless artists, writers, and musicians over the centuries, each captivated by the lake's serene beauty and changing moods. With every season, Lake Constance seems to transform, offering visitors a reason to return time and again: summers bring sailing and festivals, autumns dazzle with the colors of vineyards in harvest, winters offer a peaceful retreat, and spring unfolds in a burst of blossoms.

For those planning their first visit, it's useful to know a few essentials about Lake Constance. The lake's unique position on the borders of three countries offers an international travel experience within a single region. Although each side of the lake brings its own distinct cultural flavor, the ease of traveling between Germany, Austria, and Switzerland makes Lake Constance an accessible and seamless destination for all kinds of travelers.

The best time to visit largely depends on the experience you're after. For sun-seekers and swimmers, June to September promises warmer

temperatures and lively shores filled with outdoor activities. During the summer, you'll find opportunities for boating, windsurfing, hiking, and even open-air festivals celebrating everything from wine to classical music. Autumn brings a quieter, more introspective beauty to the lake, ideal for those who enjoy nature hikes and local harvests. If you're visiting during winter, the lake exudes a calm, almost magical stillness, perfect for relaxation and exploring charming Christmas markets with the Alps as a backdrop. Spring, with its blooming orchards and budding vineyards, signals a fresh beginning and is perfect for sightseeing without the crowds.

When it comes to getting around, visitors can rely on an excellent network of ferries and trains that connect major towns around the lake, making it easy to explore without a car. For those who love cycling, Lake Constance offers one of Europe's most scenic bike paths, the Bodensee-Radweg, which allows travelers to experience the region at a leisurely pace while connecting with the natural landscape. And don't forget: no visit to Lake Constance is complete without a boat trip to fully appreciate the lake's scale and the views of the surrounding countryside.

Beyond its stunning scenery, Lake Constance is a melting pot of cultural influences. Each town and village around the lake has its own unique identity, from the medieval streets of Konstanz to the baroque architecture of Meersburg, from the historic charm of Lindau to the scenic beauty of Bregenz in Austria. Wherever you choose to start, you'll be welcomed by friendly locals who share a deep love for the region and are eager to showcase its heritage, flavors, and traditions.

In short, Lake Constance isn't just a destination—it's an experience. It's a place where you can drift on gentle waves, take in panoramic mountain views, stroll through centuries-old streets, and sip local wines in cozy cellars. It's a place that invites you to step back in time and escape the rush of modern life. So, whether you're planning a family vacation, a romantic getaway, or a solo retreat to rediscover yourself, Lake Constance has something magical waiting for you at every turn.

1.1 OVERVIEW OF LAKE CONSTANCE

Lake Constance, or "Bodensee" as it's locally known, is much more than a stunning natural attraction; it's a cultural and historical treasure that has captivated people for centuries. This lake, one of Europe's largest, is shared by Germany, Austria, and Switzerland, creating a unique blend of landscapes and traditions along its shores. With a length of about 63 kilometers and an expansive shoreline, Lake Constance has served as a vital hub for trade, settlement, and cultural exchange for millennia.

History

The history of Lake Constance is a fascinating story shaped by the civilizations that flourished around its waters. Roman settlements were some of the earliest organized communities here, with archaeologists uncovering remains of Roman baths, villas, and roads, attesting to the lake's early significance as a trading post. The medieval period brought the growth of towns and cities, with Konstanz becoming a powerful center for trade and religion. In fact, the famous Council of Constance was held here in the early

15th century, a pivotal event in Catholic history.

Over the centuries, towns like Meersburg, Lindau, and Bregenz developed their own unique cultures, each contributing to the rich heritage that still defines the lake region today.

Geography

The geography of Lake Constance is as captivating as its history. Situated at the northern edge of the Alps, the lake is bordered by gentle hills, fertile vineyards, and towering mountains. The lake itself is divided into two main parts: the Upper Lake (Obersee) and the Lower Lake (Untersee), with the River Rhine acting as both the inflow and outflow. This unique setup makes Lake Constance a prime spot for various outdoor activities, from water sports to mountain hiking, and provides some of the most scenic views in Central Europe. The shores are dotted with charming towns and villages, where visitors can immerse themselves in the idyllic surroundings, relax by the water, or explore lush landscapes by foot, bike, or boat.

Significance

Lake Constance has long been a place where people come to connect—with nature, with history, and with each other. The lake's central location and multicultural surroundings make it a vibrant and culturally diverse area. Locals take immense pride in the lake, celebrating its importance through festivals, conservation efforts, and a dedication to sustainable tourism. For centuries, it has inspired poets, artists, and musicians, its serene beauty reflecting the alpine peaks above and creating an almost magical quality that draws travelers from all over the world. Today, Lake Constance remains a testament to the harmonious blend of natural beauty and cultural heritage, making it a must-visit for anyone looking to explore one of Europe's hidden gems.

1.2 ESSENTIAL TRAVEL INFORMATION

Lake Constance is a year-round destination, each season offering something unique for visitors. The lake's versatile climate and location mean you can enjoy both warm, activity-filled summers and peaceful, snow-kissed winters, depending on your preferences.

When to Visit

Choosing the best time to visit Lake Constance depends on the type of experience you're after. Summer (June to September) is by far the most popular season, drawing crowds who come for the warm weather, festivals, and endless outdoor activities. Temperatures are typically comfortable, ranging between 20°C and 28°C (68°F to 82°F), perfect for swimming, boating, or enjoying a scenic bike ride around the lake. The summer months also bring lively festivals, including the Bregenz Festival with its iconic floating stage, adding a unique cultural flavor to any visit.

Spring (March to May) and autumn (October to November) are ideal for those who prefer a quieter atmosphere. In spring, the surrounding orchards and vineyards are in full bloom, painting the landscape in pastel shades of pink, green, and yellow. Autumn, on the other hand, is harvest season, and visitors can sample fresh local produce and attend wine festivals celebrating the lake's vibrant wine-making traditions. Both seasons have cooler temperatures, ranging between 10°C and 20°C (50°F to 68°F), making them perfect for sightseeing, hiking, and immersing in local culture without the high-season crowds.

Winter (December to February) brings a completely different charm to Lake Constance. The area becomes a peaceful retreat where visitors can experience a slower pace, cozying up in lakeside villages and enjoying Christmas markets, particularly in places like Lindau and Konstanz. Temperatures hover around freezing, with occasional snowfall that transforms the landscape into a winter wonderland. This is also the season for spa experiences, as well as skiing in nearby Alpine resorts for those willing to take a short drive from the lake.

Climate and Travel Tips

Lake Constance enjoys a mild climate for much of the year, but it's always wise to pack according to the season and plan for sudden weather changes. Summers can occasionally bring thunderstorms, so a light rain jacket or umbrella can be useful. If you're visiting in spring or autumn, layering is key since mornings and evenings tend to be cooler than the afternoons. Winter travelers should bring warm clothing and sturdy shoes for icy paths, especially if exploring on foot.

When it comes to getting around, the Lake

Constance region is highly accessible by public transport. Ferries, trains, and buses connect major towns around the lake, making it easy to explore without a car. For a more scenic approach, many travelers opt for biking or boating, both of which offer a relaxing way to take in the lake's natural beauty. A popular choice is the Bodensee-Radweg, a 270-kilometer cycling path that circles the lake, offering stunning views at every turn.

Overall, whether you're seeking outdoor adventure, historical exploration, or peaceful relaxation, Lake Constance offers something unique in every season. With a bit of planning and the right timing, your visit to this enchanting region can be truly unforgettable.

CHAPTER 2

GETTING TO LAKE CONSTANCE

Embarking on a journey to Lake Constance is the first step toward discovering one of Europe's hidden gems. Whether you're a seasoned traveler or venturing out on your first adventure, getting to this stunning region is a straightforward and enjoyable process that sets the tone for the experiences awaiting you. This chapter will guide you through the various transportation options, highlighting the best ways to arrive and ensuring that your trip begins smoothly and stress-free.

Lake Constance, or Bodensee as it is known in German, is well-connected to major cities and transportation hubs in Germany, Austria, and Switzerland, making it an accessible destination for visitors from all corners of the globe. The region is a beautiful blend of natural beauty and cultural richness, and the journey to get there can be just as memorable as the destination itself. With its breathtaking views of the Alps, charming towns, and the shimmering waters of the lake, the approach to Lake Constance is a feast for the senses.

Travelers can choose from a variety of modes of

transportation to reach the lake, depending on where they are coming from and their personal preferences. From international airports in Zurich, Munich, and Friedrichshafen to train networks that crisscross the region, there are multiple entry points that offer convenient access to the lake and its surroundings. For those who enjoy the road, driving can be a delightful way to explore the scenic landscapes, with picturesque routes that meander through quaint villages and rolling vineyards.

Once you arrive, the options for getting around the area are just as diverse. Public transportation, including trains and buses, offers a reliable means to explore towns and attractions around the lake. For a more leisurely experience, consider renting a bike or taking a ferry ride, allowing you to soak in the stunning views of the water and the picturesque shoreline.

In this chapter, we will delve deeper into the various travel options, including detailed information about public transport schedules, tips for driving in the region, and insights into the best airports to fly into.

Whether you prefer the ease of train travel or the adventure of a scenic drive, we'll ensure you have all the information you need to make your journey to Lake Constance as enjoyable as the destination itself.

Prepare to immerse yourself in the beauty and charm of Lake Constance. With a little planning and an adventurous spirit, your journey to this remarkable region will not only be the start of your exploration but also a delightful experience in its own right. Let's embark on this journey together!

2.1 TRANSPORTATION OPTIONS

Getting to Lake Constance is an exciting part of the journey, and the region offers a variety of transportation options to suit every traveler's needs. Whether you prefer the speed of air travel, the convenience of trains, or the freedom of driving, there's a way to reach this beautiful area that fits your style.

Flights:

For international travelers, the nearest major airports are Zurich Airport (ZRH) in Switzerland, Munich Airport (MUC) in Germany, and Friedrichshafen Airport (FDH) in Germany. Zurich is particularly well-connected, with numerous international flights arriving daily. From Zurich, you can take a scenic train ride to Lake Constance, which takes around 1.5 hours and offers stunning views of the countryside along the way. Munich Airport, located about two hours from the lake, also provides good train connections. Friedrichshafen Airport is the closest to the lake and is ideal for those coming from within Europe, though it has a smaller range of flights. Once at any of these airports, rental cars and shuttle services are available for those who prefer a more direct route to their destination.

Trains:

Germany, Austria, and Switzerland have a

well-developed and efficient train network that makes traveling to Lake Constance a breeze. Major cities like Munich, Stuttgart, and Zurich offer direct train connections to towns around the lake, such as Konstanz, Lindau, and Meersburg. The trains are comfortable, clean, and often equipped with scenic panoramic windows, allowing you to enjoy the beautiful landscapes en route. In particular, the train journey from Zurich to Lake Constance is renowned for its breathtaking views of the Alps and the sparkling waters of the lake as you draw nearer.

Road Access:

For those who enjoy driving, reaching Lake Constance by car is an excellent choice. The region is easily accessible via the A81 and A8 motorways in Germany, as well as other well-maintained roads connecting Austria and Switzerland. Driving offers the flexibility to explore at your own pace, stopping at charming villages and vineyards along the way. Plus, the journey through the rolling hills and vineyards can be just as captivating as the lake itself. Just remember to familiarize yourself with local driving laws and regulations, as they may differ from what you're used to.

2.2 NAVIGATING THE REGION

Once you've arrived at Lake Constance, navigating the region is equally straightforward, with a variety of options to explore its beauty.

Public Transportation:
The public transportation system around Lake Constance is efficient and user-friendly, making it easy to get from one charming town to

another. The region is served by local buses and trains that connect the key destinations around the lake. The trains run frequently, and schedules are usually punctual, allowing for seamless transfers between towns. For instance, you can easily hop on a train from Konstanz to Meersburg or Lindau, soaking in the lovely scenery along the way. Additionally, the Bodensee-Oberschwaben Verkehrsverbund (bodo) network offers a unified ticketing system that allows for convenient transfers between different modes of transport, saving you both time and money.

Bike Rentals:

For a more intimate experience of the area, consider renting a bike. Lake Constance is known for its extensive cycling paths, with routes that weave along the lakeshore and through picturesque landscapes. Cycling not only provides a healthy way to explore but also allows you to pause and appreciate the stunning views at your own pace. Many towns around the lake offer bike rental services, making it easy to grab a bike and set off on your adventure. Whether you're a seasoned cyclist or a casual rider, you'll find paths suitable for all levels.

Ferry Services:

The ferry services at Lake Constance add a unique dimension to your travel experience. With regular ferry connections between towns like Meersburg, Konstanz, and Lindau, you can explore the lake in a relaxed manner, enjoying the stunning vistas from the water. The ferries are a popular choice for both locals and tourists, offering a delightful way to see the shoreline from a different perspective.

There's something magical about cruising across the shimmering lake, with the majestic mountains in the background and the gentle waves lapping against the hull. Whether you're commuting to another town or simply taking a scenic cruise, the ferries are a fantastic option to include in your travel plans.

In summary, whether you arrive by plane, train, or car, and however you choose to get around, Lake Constance offers an array of transportation options that ensure your journey is smooth and enjoyable. With easy access and diverse ways to explore the region, you'll find that getting to and around this beautiful area is as pleasurable as the experiences that await you.

CHAPTER 3

TOP ATTRACTIONS AROUND LAKE CONSTANCE

Lake Constance is a region that brims with beauty, history, and endless surprises at every corner, offering a blend of attractions that appeal to every type of traveler. Whether you're drawn to medieval castles, sweeping vineyard views, or charming old towns, there's something here to capture your heart. Each stop along the lake's shores offers a window into the area's cultural heritage, natural wonders, and unique local experiences that have defined this place for centuries. From historic cathedrals to scenic islands, from modern art galleries to ancient ruins, Lake Constance is more than just a destination—it's a journey that speaks to all of your senses.

The Timeless Charm of Constance (Konstanz)

The town of Constance, located at the western tip of Lake Constance, is a perfect starting point for exploring the area. With its cobbled streets, medieval buildings, and captivating views, Constance feels like a storybook town brought to life. Walking through the city, you'll be greeted by the proud facades of houses dating back hundreds of years, each seemingly whispering tales of the past. Constance played a pivotal role in European history, most famously hosting the Council of Constance from 1414 to 1418, a historical turning point for the Catholic Church.

The Constance Cathedral, with its towering spires and intricate carvings, is a must-visit landmark, offering both stunning architecture and panoramic views of the city and lake from its tower.

Constance is also home to the Sea Life Aquarium, which invites visitors into the mysterious underwater world of Lake Constance and beyond. This is an especially popular stop for families and those interested in marine life, providing an engaging look at local ecosystems and the creatures that inhabit them. After a day of exploring, the town's bustling harbor area is the perfect place to relax, enjoy a coffee, and watch the boats glide across the water.

Mainau Island – The Flowering Jewel of Lake Constance

If there's one attraction you can't miss, it's the enchanting Mainau Island. Known as the "Flower Island," Mainau is a horticultural masterpiece that bursts into color with each season. Picture yourself wandering through gardens filled with rare orchids, vibrant roses, and lush Mediterranean plants, all meticulously arranged to create a paradise that feels almost dreamlike. Mainau Island isn't just a garden; it's an immersive experience where the beauty of nature and careful artistry blend to create a feast for the senses.

This 45-hectare island also offers more than just botanical wonders. Mainau is home to a historic baroque palace, once the summer residence of the Swedish royal family. The palace's interior is a walk back in time, adorned with period furniture and artworks that showcase the grandeur of a bygone era. For families, Mainau features a petting zoo, butterfly house, and various activities to keep younger visitors entertained, making it a perfect spot for a memorable day out with loved ones. Spring and summer are especially magical times to visit, but each season on Mainau brings something unique.

The Majesty of Meersburg Castle

Meersburg, located on the German shore of Lake Constance, is a town that perfectly balances medieval charm and natural beauty. Its crowning jewel is Meersburg Castle, which towers over the town with its formidable walls and ancient towers. As one of Germany's oldest inhabited castles, Meersburg Castle offers visitors a truly immersive experience. Walking through the castle's halls, dungeons, and grand rooms, you can almost feel the presence of the nobles, knights, and courtiers who once lived within these walls. With its imposing stone walls, narrow staircases, and sweeping lake views, the castle is a journey back to the Middle Ages, capturing the romance and intrigue of a time when fortresses dominated the landscape.

Besides its historical allure, Meersburg offers stunning views over vineyards that stretch down to the lake's edge, where winemakers have been perfecting their craft for centuries. A stroll through Meersburg's cobblestone streets reveals half-timbered houses, quaint cafés, and local shops selling handcrafted souvenirs. Be sure to try some local wine, especially the crisp white wines for which the region is known, while enjoying a breathtaking view of Lake Constance.

The Cultural Hub of Bregenz

On the Austrian side of the lake lies Bregenz, a city that's both a cultural epicenter and a scenic retreat. Famous for its annual Bregenz Festival, which draws art and music lovers from around the world, Bregenz is the ideal destination for those with a love for the arts. The Bregenz Festival's floating stage, set against the stunning backdrop of Lake Constance, hosts world-class opera and musical performances, offering a viewing experience like no other. The sight of a grand production set against the evening sky, with the lake shimmering in the background, is unforgettable.

Beyond the festival, Bregenz is known for the Pfänder Mountain, which rises majestically above the town and offers some of the best panoramic views in the region. A quick cable car ride takes you to the summit, where hiking trails, observation points, and a small zoo await. From here, you can gaze across Lake Constance, with the Alps forming a spectacular frame, creating a view that leaves an indelible impression.

Lindau – A Lakeside Paradise

The island town of Lindau, located on the eastern shore of Lake Constance, is a destination that perfectly balances history, leisure, and natural beauty. Lindau's Old Town, connected to the mainland by a bridge, is a maze of charming alleyways, medieval towers, and historic buildings. The town's harbor, watched over by a lion statue and a lighthouse, is one of the most picturesque scenes on Lake Constance, offering incredible photo opportunities and a serene setting to watch the sunset.

Lindau is also a hub for water-based activities, with plenty of options for sailing, swimming, and lake cruises. The relaxed, island-like atmosphere makes it easy to lose track of time as you wander its narrow streets, sip coffee in a cozy café, or browse local artisan shops. The architecture reflects a blend of German, Austrian, and Swiss influences, embodying the multicultural spirit of the lake region.

From the flower-filled paradise of Mainau Island to the historical depths of Meersburg Castle, Lake Constance offers an endless array of attractions that tell the story of the region's past, present, and future. Each destination around the lake has its own character, each landmark its own story, and every visit brings a new perspective to this remarkable area. Here, you're not just a tourist; you're a participant in a rich tradition of exploration and appreciation that has endured for centuries. Whether your journey takes you to historic landmarks, scenic viewpoints, or vibrant cultural centers, Lake Constance has something extraordinary waiting for you at every turn.

3.1 HISTORIC TOWNS AND VILLAGES

Exploring the shores of Lake Constance offers more than beautiful views; it's a journey through history preserved in the charming towns and villages that line the lake. Each town, with its own distinct personality, showcases a unique piece of the area's culture, history, and beauty.

Starting with **Konstanz**, this vibrant city on the western shore of Lake Constance is the largest on the lake and a true gateway to its wonders. Stepping into Konstanz is like entering a living museum. The medieval Old Town is rich with narrow streets, historic buildings, and fascinating tales. Wandering through its cobblestone alleys, you'll encounter the majestic Konstanz Cathedral, whose origins date back over a thousand years. The Cathedral's tower offers sweeping views of the lake, rewarding visitors who make the climb with a breathtaking sight. Konstanz is also home to the famous Imperia statue, a 30-foot-high sculpture that gracefully rotates and reflects the town's intriguing history.

The city's historical significance is notable, too, as it hosted the Council of Constance from 1414 to 1418, a pivotal event for the Catholic Church. Konstanz combines history with a modern flair, boasting cozy cafes, restaurants, and shops that bring a touch of contemporary energy to this ancient city.

Next, **Lindau** is a picturesque Bavarian town located on a small island on the eastern shore of Lake Constance, connected to the mainland by a narrow bridge. Lindau's harbor is a vision, marked by the iconic stone lion and a 33-meter lighthouse that stands guard over the lake. This harbor scene is one of the most photographed views in the entire region and embodies the spirit of Lake Constance's beauty. Lindau's Old Town is a treasure trove of half-timbered houses, medieval facades, and enchanting alleyways. As you walk through the town, you can almost feel the whispers of the past that have shaped this beautiful island. Lindau also offers several delightful squares and fountains where locals and visitors gather, providing an ideal spot to take in the charming atmosphere of this lakeside paradise.

Finally, **Meersburg** is a fairytale town famous for its medieval charm. Set against the hills on the northern shore, it's impossible not to be captivated by its historic architecture and dramatic castle, known as Meersburg Castle. One of the oldest castles still inhabited in Germany, Meersburg Castle invites visitors to walk through centuries of history. Inside, you'll find an impressive collection of artifacts, from knightly armor to ancient tapestries, each piece telling a story of the castle's storied past. Beyond the castle, Meersburg's narrow streets and brightly colored houses make for a delightful stroll, with every corner offering a view of the lake or surrounding vineyards. The lower part of town, near the water, is perfect for a leisurely walk, with quaint cafes and local wine tastings that introduce visitors to the region's deep wine-making traditions. Meersburg is truly a living postcard, preserving the allure of medieval life with all the comforts of today.

Together, Konstanz, Lindau, and Meersburg represent the historic heart of Lake Constance. Each town holds its own special charm, and visiting all three offers a rich perspective on the lake's enduring legacy.

3.2 CULTURAL SITES AND MUSEUMS

Lake Constance is a cultural treasure trove, home to museums and galleries that reveal the stories, art, and heritage of this diverse region. These cultural sites provide visitors with an intimate look at the lake's multifaceted history, artistic heritage, and the various influences that have shaped the region over centuries.

A must-see cultural gem in the area is the **Rosgarten Museum in Konstanz**, which presents an extensive collection of artifacts that tell the story of Konstanz and the surrounding region. Housed in a former guild hall, the Rosgarten Museum provides insights into the social, cultural, and political history of the area, from medieval times through the Renaissance and beyond. Exhibits range from traditional clothing and household items to weapons and tools, offering a tangible connection to the past. This museum allows visitors to envision life in Konstanz over the ages, making it a perfect stop for history enthusiasts.

In Meersburg, the **Vineyard Museum** offers a delightful exploration of the area's deep-rooted wine-making traditions. Located in a historic building, the museum guides you through the process of winemaking as it's been practiced in the

Lake Constance region for centuries. Exhibits include ancient winemaking equipment, historical documents, and, of course, the opportunity to taste some of the region's famous white wines. This museum is more than just a look at wine; it's a look at the agricultural heritage of Lake Constance and the families who have cultivated the land for generations.

For art lovers, the **Kunstmuseum (Art Museum) in Bregenz**, on the Austrian side of the lake, is a contemporary art museum that showcases innovative works from both Austrian and international artists. Known for its striking modern architecture and rotating exhibitions, the Kunstmuseum Bregenz attracts visitors who appreciate modern design and thought-provoking art. The museum's exhibitions often tackle themes of identity, nature, and society, creating a fascinating dialogue between the artwork and the viewer. Set against the backdrop of Lake Constance, this museum is a cultural highlight that contrasts beautifully with the historical attractions in the area.

Another captivating cultural site is **Reichenau Island**, a UNESCO World Heritage site. Known for its monastic history, Reichenau Island was home to a thriving monastic community in the early Middle Ages, and its preserved medieval churches are a marvel to visit. The Romanesque churches of St. George, St. Peter and Paul, and the Reichenau Abbey offer glimpses into medieval religious art and architecture, and each is adorned with ancient frescoes that have survived for over a thousand years. Reichenau is not only a place of historic significance but also a serene spot for reflection, as the island's peaceful environment transports visitors to a simpler time.

These cultural sites around Lake Constance provide a diverse look at the area's heritage. Whether you're diving into history at the Rosgarten Museum, experiencing modern art at Kunstmuseum Bregenz, or discovering centuries-old winemaking techniques at the Vineyard Museum, each visit deepens your understanding of the Lake Constance region. Together, these museums, galleries, and heritage sites offer travelers a well-rounded cultural experience, allowing them to appreciate the unique blend of history, art, and tradition that makes Lake Constance such an extraordinary destination.

CHAPTER 4

NATURE AND OUTDOOR ACTIVITIES

Lake Constance is more than a picturesque body of water; it's a natural haven brimming with endless opportunities for adventure and relaxation in the great outdoors. Surrounded by breathtaking landscapes, lush forests, and towering mountains, this region invites travelers to step out of their routines and into nature's embrace. From serene lake shores to rugged mountain trails, Lake Constance offers something for every type of outdoor enthusiast, making it the ultimate destination for nature lovers and adventure seekers alike.

Imagine starting your morning with the gentle lapping of waves against the shore, the cool air fresh with the scent of pine trees, and the sight of sun-drenched mountains in the distance. This is the daily reality around Lake Constance, where the call of the wild blends seamlessly with the comforts of civilization.

Whether you're an avid hiker, a cyclist looking for scenic routes, a water sports enthusiast, or someone seeking peace in nature's quiet corners, this chapter will guide you to the best outdoor experiences the region has to offer.

One of the most remarkable aspects of Lake Constance is its versatility. The landscape shifts dramatically from one side of the lake to the other, offering an array of environments to explore. The northern shore, bordered by Germany, is lush and gentle, with rolling hills and peaceful meadows that invite leisurely walks and bike rides. To the south, where Switzerland's Alps rise up, the terrain becomes more rugged, ideal for hikers seeking a challenge and adventurers craving the thrill of alpine landscapes. Austria, with its unique cultural and natural heritage, adds yet another dimension to the region's outdoor offerings.

For those drawn to the water, Lake Constance itself is an outdoor paradise. The lake is vast and welcoming, ideal for a variety of water-based activities. Kayaking along its shores provides a unique perspective of the region, allowing you to take in views of medieval towns, vineyards, and mountains from the gentle swells of the water.

Sailing is another popular pastime here, with the wind carrying you across the lake's crystal-clear surface, creating a sense of freedom and connection to nature. For a more relaxed day, the beaches around Lake Constance offer the perfect spots for sunbathing, picnicking, or simply enjoying a swim in the lake's refreshingly cool waters.

On land, the options are equally diverse. The region boasts an extensive network of hiking and biking trails that wind through some of Europe's most captivating scenery. The famous **Bodensee-Rundweg** (Lake Constance Circular Path) allows hikers and cyclists to explore the entire perimeter of the lake, immersing themselves in its natural beauty at every turn.

This route, stretching over 270 kilometers, takes you through dense forests, quaint villages, and peaceful vineyards, each step revealing a new facet of the region's charm. Whether you take on a small section of the trail or complete the full circuit, the Bodensee-Rundweg is an unforgettable experience that highlights the best of Lake Constance's natural wonders.

But the region's allure doesn't end with the lake and its immediate surroundings. Venture a bit further, and you'll find yourself at the foot of the Alps, where hiking trails lead to stunning vistas, crystal-clear alpine lakes, and cozy mountain huts offering a taste of local cuisine and culture. In the winter, the nearby mountains transform into a winter wonderland, attracting skiers and snowboarders from all over Europe. Cross-country skiing and snowshoeing are also popular ways to experience the snowy beauty of the area, making Lake Constance a year-round destination for outdoor activities.

Nature lovers will also appreciate the region's commitment to preserving its unique ecosystems. Lake Constance is home to several protected nature reserves, such as the

Wollmatinger Ried near Konstanz, which hosts a rich array of bird species and wetlands teeming with life. Birdwatchers and wildlife enthusiasts can wander these peaceful areas, where rare birds and animals find sanctuary, making it an ideal spot to observe nature in its purest form. These protected areas not only offer a haven for flora and fauna but also provide visitors with a chance to reconnect with the natural world in a meaningful way.

Lake Constance's outdoor offerings aren't just about adrenaline or scenic views; they're about immersing oneself in a landscape that feels timeless and untouched. Whether you're here for adventure, relaxation, or a bit of both, the natural beauty of Lake Constance creates a sense of renewal. It's a place where the pace of life slows down, allowing you to appreciate the simple pleasures of being outdoors—breathing fresh air, feeling the warmth of the sun, and marveling at the majesty of the mountains and the lake itself.

In this chapter, we'll guide you through the best nature experiences and outdoor activities around Lake Constance. From tranquil lakeside strolls to exhilarating mountain adventures, the possibilities are as vast as the lake itself. Whether you're planning an active holiday or just looking to unwind in nature's embrace, Lake Constance promises an outdoor experience you'll carry with you long after you've left its shores.

4.1 HIKING AND BIKING TRAILS

Lake Constance is renowned for its breathtaking trails that invite both hikers and bikers to explore the area's natural beauty at their own pace. Here, the landscape itself feels alive, offering a blend of gentle lakeside paths, rolling hills, and challenging mountainous routes—all with panoramic views that keep adventurers coming back for more. Whether you're a seasoned trekker seeking a strenuous climb or a casual cyclist wanting a relaxed ride, Lake Constance offers trails that fit every skill level and preference.

One of the most famous routes is the **Bodensee-Radweg**, or the Lake Constance Cycle Path, which circles the entire lake and stretches across Germany, Austria, and Switzerland. This path, spanning over 260 kilometers, is particularly popular among cyclists and offers an ever-changing backdrop of serene lake waters, charming villages, and lush vineyards. The trail winds through bustling towns like Lindau and Konstanz, where cyclists can take breaks to enjoy local cuisine, visit historic landmarks, and immerse themselves in the culture of the region. The terrain is mostly flat, making it accessible for families and less experienced cyclists, while still providing spectacular views of the lake and surrounding mountains.

For those who prefer hiking, Lake Constance is a dream destination. The **Pfänder Mountain Trail** is a must for anyone craving sweeping views of the lake with the Alps as a dramatic backdrop. Located near Bregenz in Austria, the Pfänder Mountain offers a network of trails that range from moderate to challenging, rewarding hikers with awe-inspiring vistas at nearly every turn. As you ascend, the air becomes crisper, and the lake shimmers below, offering a tranquil yet exhilarating experience. At the summit, visitors can enjoy the viewpoint, have a meal at a cozy mountain hut, or even visit the alpine wildlife park. This trail is perfect for those who want to combine physical activity with unforgettable scenery.

Another unmissable option for hikers is the **Seegang Trail**, stretching from Konstanz to Überlingen.

This trail takes you along the northern shore of

the lake, meandering through pristine forests, rolling vineyards, and quaint lakeside villages. The route has both steep sections and gentle paths, making it a well-rounded hike that offers stunning views of the water and the surrounding landscapes. Passing through protected nature reserves, the Seegang Trail also provides a chance to spot local wildlife and appreciate the region's commitment to conservation. It's a perfect blend of natural beauty and historical charm, with each village and viewpoint adding a unique touch to the journey.

4.2 WATER SPORTS AND LAKE ACTIVITIES

Lake Constance is not just a sight to admire from the shore—it's a playground for water sports enthusiasts and anyone looking to dip into the refreshing blue. With clean, calm waters and a variety of activities to choose from, the lake is perfect for summer adventures or relaxing, sun-soaked days.

Swimming is one of the simplest pleasures at Lake Constance, with plenty of designated swimming areas and hidden coves where the water is invitingly clear and calm. Many of the local beaches, such as **Strandbad Horn** near Konstanz, offer excellent facilities, including changing rooms, sunbathing areas, and cafes. The lake's shallow areas warm up nicely in the summer, creating ideal conditions for families with children, while more secluded spots provide peaceful escapes for those seeking a quiet swim surrounded by nature.

For those interested in boating, Lake Constance is a dream come true. Sailboats and motorboats dot the water, offering different ways to experience the lake's vast expanse. You can rent a boat for the day or join a guided cruise that takes you around the lake's most scenic spots. Sailing here is particularly enchanting, with the wind filling the sails as you glide past charming lakeside towns, vineyards, and distant mountain peaks.

Many towns around the lake, such as Lindau and Bregenz, offer boat rental services and guided excursions, making it easy for visitors to enjoy the water. Kayaking is also popular, providing a more intimate and hands-on way to explore Lake Constance's shoreline and get closer to its hidden inlets and serene bays.

Paddleboarding has recently become a favorite activity around Lake Constance, combining a full-body workout with the joy of being on the water. The calm sections of the lake, especially around the beaches and bays, are perfect for beginners, while more experienced paddleboarders can venture further out to explore the lake's quieter areas. Paddleboarding offers a unique perspective, standing on the water with the full panorama of the lake and mountains before you. Many lakeside towns offer rental services, so you don't need to bring your own board. Plus, the thrill of balancing and paddling adds an extra layer of fun, whether you're trying it for the first time or you're already an expert.

Lake Constance's water activities aren't just about the sport—they're about embracing the lake's tranquil spirit and experiencing the sense of freedom that comes with being surrounded by nature's vast beauty.

CHAPTER 5

EXPLORING LAKE CONSTANCE BY BOAT

To truly experience the magic of Lake Constance, there's no better way than by taking to its sparkling waters. Exploring Lake Constance by boat opens up an entirely new perspective on the region, offering not just a mode of transport but an adventure in itself. With the gentle rhythm of the waves beneath you, the fresh lake breeze in your face, and the picturesque landscapes unfolding around you, every journey across the lake becomes a memory waiting to happen.

A vast and vibrant lake bordered by three countries—Germany, Austria, and Switzerland—Lake Constance offers a unique mix of cultures, scenery, and experiences. From a boat, you can effortlessly move between historic towns, discover secluded coves, or simply drift along, surrounded by endless views of mountains, forests, and rolling vineyards.

The lake's crystalline waters reflect the changing skies and scenic surroundings, making every moment on the water feel timeless and serene.

One of the most enchanting aspects of a boat journey on Lake Constance is the freedom it brings. There's no rush or rigid itinerary; instead, you're free to explore at your own pace. Start your day with a morning cruise from Lindau, watching the sunrise over the distant Alps and casting a golden glow across the lake. Later, head towards Konstanz, where the town's centuries-old architecture lines the waterfront, creating a stunning scene against the natural beauty of the lake. Along the way, you might pass small islands, like the peaceful Reichenau Island or the flower-laden Mainau Island, each one inviting you to stop, explore, and lose yourself in its charm.

If you're looking for a more guided experience, Lake Constance offers a variety of boat tours and cruises that make exploring the lake both easy and unforgettable. Several companies provide sightseeing cruises with expert guides who share insights into the region's history, ecology, and culture as you pass significant landmarks. Picture yourself on a scenic sunset cruise, the sky painted in soft hues as the sun dips behind the Alps, transforming the lake into a shimmering, golden expanse. The tranquility of the water, combined with the breathtaking views, makes this an unforgettable experience for couples, families, or anyone seeking a moment of peace.

For those with a more adventurous spirit, renting a boat allows you to create your own personalized lake journey. Small motorboats, kayaks, and even classic sailboats are available for rent across the region, enabling you to explore off-the-beaten-path locations and hidden corners of the lake. Imagine setting out in a sailboat, catching the wind, and gliding effortlessly across the water, feeling both exhilaration and calm as you become one with the lake's gentle rhythm. Kayaking or paddleboarding is another intimate way to explore, letting you paddle right up to the lake's scenic shores and dive into the quiet serenity of less-crowded areas. With every stroke, you feel more connected to the lake and the natural world around you.

Lake Constance's boat culture also opens the door to culinary experiences you won't want to miss. Some boat tours offer on-board dining, featuring regional specialties and local wines, making your lake journey a feast for the senses. Enjoy fresh fish caught that very day from the lake, paired with crisp white wines produced in the vineyards surrounding Lake Constance.

Dining as you drift along the water, surrounded by sweeping views, turns a simple meal into a highlight of your trip.

As you sail from shore to shore, it's hard not to feel a sense of wonder at the region's unique blend of nature and history. With each dock you visit, each village you see from the water, and each hidden cove you uncover, Lake Constance reveals a little more of itself. Boating here is not just about reaching a destination; it's about soaking in the journey, letting the lake's calm, endless expanse fill you with a sense of timeless tranquility.

In this chapter, we'll guide you through the best ways to explore Lake Constance by boat, including information on boat rentals, popular cruising routes, and what to expect from various tour options. Whether you're seeking romance, family fun, or solo exploration, boating on Lake Constance offers a unique way to experience this enchanting region. From sunrise to sunset, every hour on the water brings a new view, a new discovery, and a lasting memory.

5.1 FERRY ROUTES AND BOAT TOURS

Lake Constance is a unique destination where exploring by water is both practical and magical. The lake's extensive ferry routes and guided boat tours make it incredibly easy to travel between towns, see famous sights, and even cross international borders—all while savoring the beauty of the surrounding landscapes. Each ferry and boat route offers its own blend of natural splendor and cultural insight, making any trip across the water a memorable journey.

One of the best-known ferry routes on Lake Constance is the line between **Konstanz** and **Meersburg**. This popular route runs year-round and serves as a convenient way for travelers to explore two of the lake's most iconic towns.

Konstanz, with its charming medieval architecture and vibrant cultural scene, contrasts with Meersburg's fairy-tale-like atmosphere, where colorful buildings and cobblestone streets feel like a step back in time. This ferry ride, which only takes about 15 minutes, offers sweeping views of both towns from the water, as well as the surrounding vineyards and forested hills.

For a longer, more scenic experience, there's the **Three-Country Cruise**—a guided boat tour that covers Germany, Austria, and Switzerland in a single day. This tour is perfect for those who want to experience the full breadth of Lake Constance's international character and varied landscapes. You'll pass through beautiful harbors, observe different architectural styles, and hear interesting commentary about the lake's history and ecology from knowledgeable guides. With stops in key towns, you have the chance to hop off, explore, and grab a bite before continuing your journey. The Three-Country Cruise lets you capture the spirit of Lake Constance in a unique way, providing a sense of the lake as a living, interconnected region that unites people and cultures.

For nature lovers, the **Island Tour** is a must. This tour stops at **Mainau Island** and **Reichenau Island**—two of Lake Constance's most beautiful and famous islands. Mainau, also known as the "Flower Island," is a paradise of gardens filled with blooms, butterflies, and towering trees, perfect for leisurely exploration. Reichenau Island, a UNESCO World Heritage site, offers a different kind of wonder with its historic monasteries and ancient vineyards, giving you a taste of the area's deep-rooted spiritual and agricultural heritage.

Whichever route or tour you choose, the boats themselves are often equipped with cozy interiors, open-air decks, and even snack bars or restaurants, so you can sit back and enjoy the views in comfort. From short, practical ferry rides to in-depth tours that reveal the lake's hidden gems, traveling Lake Constance by boat gives you a fresh perspective on this enchanting region.

5.2 TIPS FOR A SCENIC CRUISE

Planning a scenic cruise on Lake Constance isn't just about choosing a route; it's about timing, planning your stops, and knowing where to catch the best views. With a few well-chosen tips, you can make sure your journey across the lake is as beautiful and memorable as possible.

One of the most crucial aspects of a scenic cruise is **timing**. Early mornings and late afternoons are often ideal times to set out on the water, as the lake is quieter, and the lighting creates a picturesque effect over the water. If you want to see the lake at its most magical, consider a sunset cruise. As the sun dips behind the Alps, the lake transforms into a palette of orange, pink, and purple, providing a breathtaking view that's perfect for photography or simply soaking in the moment. Several boat companies offer sunset tours, which often include a glass of local wine or a small snack, making the experience feel extra special.

Choosing the **right route** can also make a big difference in your Lake Constance experience. If you're interested in seeing the lake's diverse landscapes, the route from **Lindau** to **Bregenz** is a great choice. This route takes you past the German-Austrian border, allowing you to admire Lindau's charming harbor and Bregenz's striking lakeside theater, which hosts the famous Bregenz Festival. The scenic stretch between these two towns includes views of alpine foothills and rolling vineyards, creating a blend of natural beauty that Lake Constance is known for.

If you're aiming to experience cultural and historic sites along your cruise, be sure to include **Konstanz** and **Überlingen** in your itinerary. Konstanz, with its medieval old town and the impressive Imperia statue at the harbor, gives visitors a sense of the lake's rich history. Überlingen, known for its well-preserved architecture and lakeside promenade, offers stunning views and a chance to stroll along the water. Each stop lets you get off the boat, wander, and explore, adding variety to your journey.

For a unique experience, don't miss the chance to stop at **Mainau Island** if your route includes it. Spending a couple of hours on this floral oasis allows you to admire its famous botanical gardens, explore its castle, and appreciate the island's tranquil atmosphere. Make sure to pack a camera, as Mainau is one of the most photogenic spots around the lake.

A few practical tips can also go a long way in enhancing your scenic cruise. Arriving early to your chosen departure point ensures that you get a good seat, whether you prefer to be up front, on the open deck, or near the windows for unobstructed views. Packing a light jacket is a good idea as well, as it can get breezy on the lake, especially in the evening. And don't forget your sunscreen and sunglasses—those lake reflections can be surprisingly intense on sunny days.

By carefully choosing your timing, route, and stops, you can make the most of your Lake Constance boat trip. With each wave and vista, your scenic cruise will bring you closer to the lake's beauty, history, and character, creating an experience you'll remember long after you step back on shore.

CHAPTER 6

CULINARY DELIGHTS OF LAKE CONSTANCE

Exploring Lake Constance is not only about stunning landscapes and historical towns—it's also about savoring flavors that capture the essence of this vibrant region. Lake Constance is a culinary paradise, where fresh ingredients, local traditions, and international influences combine to create a truly unique food scene. Whether you're wandering the bustling markets, relaxing at a lakeside restaurant, or visiting local farms, there's a sense of authenticity in every dish that reflects the character and history of the region. Here, eating isn't just a necessity; it's an experience that engages all your senses.

One of the highlights of Lake Constance cuisine is the incredible **freshness**. Located in a fertile region where Germany, Austria, and Switzerland meet, the area benefits from mild temperatures, rich soils, and pristine waters.

This perfect setting produces everything from ripe apples and juicy plums to fragrant herbs and an abundance of vegetables. And with the lake itself teeming with fish, you'll find an impressive variety of seafood dishes on offer, from simple grilled fish to rich, flavorful soups. Local fishermen head out early each morning, bringing back their catch to be served fresh at restaurants the same day. It's hard to beat the freshness and quality of lake fish like whitefish (felchen), perch, and pike, which feature prominently on menus around the region.

For those who want to dive into the region's flavors, **farm-to-table** dining is an essential part of the experience at Lake Constance. Many of the area's restaurants and inns partner with nearby farms and vineyards to offer dishes that highlight seasonal produce. Each season brings new tastes, from spring's tender asparagus and wild garlic to autumn's rich, earthy mushrooms and hearty root vegetables. These ingredients aren't just local; they're celebrated. In many towns, you'll come across farm shops where you can buy homemade jams, cheeses, and cured meats that have been crafted using age-old techniques. The culinary traditions here are deeply rooted in sustainable practices, creating a strong sense of place in every bite.

But it's not just about local ingredients—**Lake Constance cuisine is also infused with international influences**, particularly from Germany, Austria, and Switzerland. Each country brings its own flavors and techniques, creating a delightful mix of culinary styles. You might start your day with a classic German pretzel and end it with a creamy Swiss chocolate dessert. The influence of Bavarian, Austrian, and Swiss cuisine can be seen in the variety of dishes, from cheese-filled Spätzle (a local noodle dish) to crispy Wiener schnitzel. This blending of cultures makes every meal a bit of a surprise, as chefs put creative spins on traditional recipes, adding unique touches and flavors that keep you curious for what's next.

If you're a wine lover, Lake Constance offers some real gems. The **Bodensee Wine Region** is known for its exceptional wines, particularly white varieties like Müller-Thurgau and Pinot Blanc, which thrive in the cool climate and mineral-rich soils of the lake area.

Wine tasting here is more than just a chance to sample excellent wines—it's an invitation to connect with the landscape. The region's vineyards are often perched on hillsides overlooking the lake, offering breathtaking views while you sip a glass of crisp, refreshing wine. Many wineries offer guided tours and tastings, where you can learn about local grape-growing traditions and even pick up a few bottles to enjoy later. For those who prefer beer, local breweries are also part of the scene, crafting refreshing lagers and ales that pair perfectly with the region's hearty fare.

No culinary exploration of Lake Constance would be complete without indulging in the area's delicious **pastries and desserts**. The region is known for its apple-based treats, thanks to the many orchards surrounding the lake. A slice of apple strudel or a piece of Apfelkuchen (apple cake) served with a dollop of cream is a classic way to end a meal, especially when enjoyed with a view of the lake. You'll also find cakes made with plums, pears, and cherries, each bringing the taste of the region to life. And if you're visiting during Christmas, don't miss the chance to try the holiday cookies and mulled wine, as the towns around the lake transform with festive lights and seasonal markets.

The culinary delights of Lake Constance offer something for everyone, from food enthusiasts eager to try new flavors to those simply looking for a comforting meal after a day of sightseeing. Each dish, from the freshly caught fish to the lovingly made pastries, tells a story of the region's people, its history, and its connection to nature. As you dine around Lake Constance, you're not just eating—you're experiencing a taste of the lake itself, an invitation to savor a place where culture and cuisine come together beautifully.

6.1 LOCAL DISHES AND SPECIALTIES

When visiting Lake Constance, immersing yourself in the local cuisine is an absolute must. Here, food is a celebration of the region's natural abundance and rich culinary traditions, reflecting German, Austrian, and Swiss influences. One of the most iconic dishes to try is **Bodensee-Felchen**—a delicate, white lake fish, typically pan-fried or smoked and served with potatoes or a simple side salad. Known for its mild, buttery flavor, felchen is a staple on nearly every restaurant menu around the lake, and there's a certain magic to eating it fresh, prepared by locals who've perfected the dish over generations.

Another must-try is **Käsespätzle**, a hearty German dish resembling macaroni and cheese but with a distinct twist. These soft egg noodles are mixed with layers of gooey cheese, often topped with crispy fried onions, making it the perfect comfort food after a long day of exploring. For a touch of the Austrian influence, **Wiener Schnitzel** is another classic that finds its way to tables here, a breaded and pan-fried veal or pork cutlet served with potato salad or lingonberry jam for a sweet contrast.

Vegetable lovers will want to try dishes like **Maultaschen**—a savory German dumpling filled with spinach, minced meat, and herbs. Maultaschen are often compared to ravioli and can be enjoyed either boiled or fried, offering a satisfying taste of the region's humble, earthy ingredients. For those with a sweet tooth, **Apfelkuchen** (apple cake) or **Apfelstrudel** are local favorites, celebrating the abundance of apples from orchards around Lake Constance. Paired with whipped cream or a scoop of vanilla ice cream, these desserts bring the flavors of the region's fruit harvests to life in every bite.

The local drinks are equally inviting. **Bodensee wines**—especially the white wines like Müller-Thurgau and Pinot Blanc—are must-tries. These wines capture the crisp, mineral-rich terroir of the region, making them the perfect pairing for fresh fish or lighter dishes. Beer lovers, too, will find solace in the local brews, with German and Austrian beers widely available. And for something unique, try **Most**, a fermented apple cider, which is both refreshing and offers a true taste of the local orchards. Each of these dishes and drinks offers a story, a slice of Lake Constance life to savor.

6.2 POPULAR DINING SPOTS

Lake Constance is home to an array of dining experiences, from casual lakeside cafés to gourmet restaurants with breathtaking views. For travelers looking to sample the best local dishes, a few places stand out. **Weinstube Birnauer Oberhof** in Uhldingen-Mühlhofen, Germany, offers a cozy, authentic German dining experience.

With rustic décor and a friendly atmosphere, it's perfect for trying local specialties like Käsespätzle and Maultaschen, served in generous portions with local wines to match. The restaurant's hilltop location offers views of the lake that add a picturesque backdrop to your meal.

For a refined dining experience, **Seerestaurant Belvedere** in Hagnau, Germany, is an excellent choice. Known for its creative, seasonal dishes that highlight the lake's fish, this restaurant provides both a scenic lakeside view and a carefully curated menu. It's a favorite for locals and travelers alike, whether for a romantic evening or a leisurely lunch in the sunshine. **Gasthaus Zur Fischerin** in Romanshorn, Switzerland, is another must-visit for fish lovers. Known for its exquisite Bodensee-Felchen, it serves up the local lake fish in a variety of ways, from smoked to delicately grilled, bringing out the fresh, natural flavor of the fish.

If you're seeking a lively experience, the **Markthalle Bregenz** in Austria is a vibrant food market offering everything from artisanal cheese to baked goods and fresh produce. This market is not just for buying ingredients; it's a social hub where locals gather, food stalls tempt with a variety of snacks, and the lively atmosphere brings the flavors of the region to life. Sampling some street food here or simply browsing the stalls gives you an authentic taste of the local food culture.

For a more laid-back experience, try **Café Grossstadt** in Lindau, Germany. Known for its pastries, coffee, and quaint atmosphere, it's the perfect spot to relax and watch the world go by after a day of exploring. Their apple strudel, paired with a cup of coffee, is a must-try. **Haus zum Cavazzen** in Lindau, a beautiful building with a rich history, is also worth visiting for both its architectural beauty and its intimate restaurant offering regional favorites in a charming setting.

Whether you're dining at a fine restaurant, grabbing a quick snack at a market, or sipping coffee at a cozy café, each experience offers a delicious and memorable way to connect with Lake Constance's culture. Here, food is more than just a meal—it's an invitation to explore the region's traditions, meet its people, and experience the natural beauty that surrounds you.

CHAPTER 7

WINE AND VINEYARD TOURS

A trip to Lake Constance isn't complete without a journey through its scenic vineyards, where rolling hills are blanketed with lush vines, and every glass of wine tells a story of the land, climate, and the dedicated hands that cultivated it. In this region, wine is more than a beverage—it's a cultural experience, a link to the past, and a chance to taste the essence of Lake Constance itself. Known for its cool-climate wines, the area around the lake produces distinctive varietals that are both refreshing and deeply satisfying, making a vineyard tour one of the most rewarding experiences for any traveler.

Nestled along the lake's shores, you'll find an array of family-owned vineyards, each offering a unique perspective on the winemaking craft. As you step onto the vineyards, you're immediately greeted by rows of grapevines stretching out under the sun, often with the glistening lake in the background and the Alps towering in the distance.

Here, vintners have perfected the art of cultivating grape varieties like **Müller-Thurgau**, **Pinot Noir**, and **Pinot Blanc**, each thriving in the mineral-rich soil of the region. These wines are light, crisp, and elegant, with hints of fruit and delicate floral notes, capturing the fresh Alpine air and the unique terroir of Lake Constance.

Embarking on a wine tour around Lake Constance is about immersing yourself in local tradition and discovering the deep-rooted passion that fuels these vineyards. Most tours include a guided stroll through the vineyards, where winemakers share the secrets of their craft, from the care taken with each vine to the seasonal rituals that give life to the grapes. Walking between the vines, you'll learn about the unique microclimate created by the lake, which gently tempers temperatures and creates ideal conditions for winemaking. You may even get to sample grapes right off the vine, appreciating the balance of sweetness and acidity that will eventually define the wine's character.

The real highlight, of course, is the tasting itself.

Often held in charming, rustic cellars or scenic terraces overlooking the lake, these tastings introduce you to the best of Lake Constance's wine offerings. Sipping a chilled glass of Müller-Thurgau or a fruity Pinot Noir, you'll feel the expertise of generations in each taste, with flavors that are at once crisp and complex, clean and vibrant. The local wine has a character unlike any other—a true reflection of the landscape and the care with which it was crafted. Each vineyard has its own signature notes and styles, so as you tour several wineries, you'll come to appreciate the subtle variations that make each bottle unique.

For many, the most memorable part of these tours is the chance to connect with the winemakers themselves. Many of the vineyards around Lake Constance are family-owned, with traditions passed down through generations. Here, vintners welcome you with genuine warmth and enthusiasm, sharing stories about their families, the land, and the challenges and triumphs of winemaking. It's a rare opportunity to gain insight into the life and passion of the people who bring these wines to life.

Whether you're a wine connoisseur or simply a curious traveler, a vineyard tour around Lake Constance offers an intimate, enriching experience that will deepen your appreciation for wine. These tours are not just about tasting but about slowing down, taking in the scenery, and connecting with the very heart of the region. And as you leave with a bottle or two of your favorites, you're taking a piece of Lake Constance's legacy with you—a reminder of your time among the vines and the memories crafted in this picturesque lakeside paradise.

7.1 INTRODUCTION TO LOCAL WINE

Lake Constance, nestled at the crossroads of Germany, Austria, and Switzerland, is more than just a stunning destination; it's also home to a rich wine culture that's deeply intertwined with the region's identity. Here, winemaking dates back to Roman times, and the area's vineyards are known for producing wines that beautifully capture the essence of this unique environment.

The region's cool climate and mineral-rich soil

give rise to a delicate and refreshing style of wine that's light, crisp, and vibrant—a perfect match for the lakeside landscape and lifestyle.

The lake itself plays an essential role in the success of these vineyards. Acting as a natural temperature regulator, Lake Constance protects vines from extreme weather, creating a microclimate that allows grapes to ripen slowly and develop a complex flavor profile. This natural cooling effect results in wines that are full of nuanced flavors, balancing fruitiness with a crisp acidity that makes them refreshing and versatile. The **Müller-Thurgau** grape, known for its light body and notes of apple and pear, is the region's standout white wine, embodying the fresh, clean character of Lake Constance. Another favorite is **Pinot Noir** (locally called Spätburgunder), which thrives here, resulting in a light yet flavorful red with hints of berries and spices, perfectly suited for the area's cuisine and climate.

Lake Constance's wine culture goes beyond simply producing wine; it's a way of life. Each bottle reflects a story of heritage, tradition, and respect for nature. Locals celebrate their wine with pride, and many festivals, like the Lake Constance Wine Festival, are held throughout the year to honor the harvest and showcase the diverse offerings from around the lake. For visitors, this love of wine provides a fantastic opportunity to connect with the region, tasting wines that truly represent the land and its people. A glass of Lake Constance wine is more than a drink; it's an invitation to savor a part of the region's soul.

7.2 TOP WINERIES TO VISIT

Exploring the wineries around Lake Constance offers an unforgettable journey through some of the region's most scenic and inviting landscapes. Each winery has its own personality and charm, from traditional family-owned vineyards to larger, established estates, and each offers a unique experience for visitors.

Weingut Aufricht, near Meersburg, is one of the top choices, known for its idyllic setting overlooking the lake and for producing a stellar selection of Müller-Thurgau and Pinot Noir. Here, visitors can enjoy guided tours through the vineyards, learning about the unique climate and winemaking process. The tasting room offers panoramic views, so as you savor each sip, you're also taking in the stunning scenery that makes this winery so special.

In Hagnau, **Winzerverein Hagnau** is a must-visit, offering a blend of history, innovation, and community spirit. It's one of the oldest cooperative wineries in Germany, where local winegrowers pool their harvests to create wines that embody the spirit of collaboration. Tours here take you behind the scenes, allowing you to learn how the cooperative system works and why it's been so successful in producing award-winning wines. Tasting at Winzerverein Hagnau feels like a celebration of the area's close-knit community, where each bottle tells a collective story of the families who've worked these vineyards for generations.

If you're in the mood for something intimate and artisanal, **Weingut Markgraf von Baden** in Salem is a smaller, family-owned estate with a reputation for excellent wines. This winery combines traditional methods with a passion for sustainable agriculture, focusing on low-intervention techniques that bring out the purity of the grapes. Tours here often include a walk through the vines and a tasting in their cozy cellar, where you can savor wines crafted with care and precision. This estate is known for its Riesling and Pinot Blanc, both of which beautifully showcase the minerality of Lake Constance's terroir.

For those who prefer a more hands-on experience, **Weinbaumuseum Meersburg** offers the chance to step back in time and learn about the historical roots of winemaking in the region. The museum provides interactive displays and artifacts that trace the evolution of viticulture around Lake Constance, making it a fascinating stop for history buffs and wine lovers alike.

You can also taste a selection of wines here,

pairing the experience with the knowledge you've just gained about the traditions and innovations behind each bottle.

Each of these wineries offers not just a taste of the local wine but a chance to immerse yourself in the heritage, culture, and beauty of Lake Constance. Whether you're wandering through sun-dappled vineyards, chatting with passionate winemakers, or simply sipping wine as you overlook the lake, these vineyard experiences create memories that go far beyond the glass, leaving you with a true appreciation of Lake Constance's wine culture.

CHAPTER 8

CULTURAL EVENTS AND FESTIVALS

As the seasons turn and the sun casts its warm glow over Lake Constance, the region comes alive with a vibrant tapestry of cultural events and festivals that reflect its rich history, diverse traditions, and the joyful spirit of its people. From lively markets bursting with local crafts to grand celebrations of music and dance, the festivals around Lake Constance offer visitors a unique opportunity to immerse themselves in the culture and community of this enchanting area. Each event is a colorful celebration, drawing locals and travelers alike into a world of festivity, where laughter, music, and the aroma of delicious food fill the air.

The festival calendar kicks off in spring with the **Lake Constance Spring Fair**, a charming event that heralds the arrival of warmer days. Stalls brimming with handmade crafts, fresh produce, and local delicacies line the waterfront, creating a lively atmosphere filled with the sounds of laughter and chatter.

Visitors can taste artisanal cheeses, indulge in freshly baked goods, and sample local wines while enjoying live performances by regional musicians. This fair isn't just a marketplace; it's a celebration of the community's creativity and a perfect way to experience the warmth of Lake Constance's hospitality.

As summer approaches, the festivities ramp up with the renowned **Lake Constance Festival** in Konstanz. This week-long event transforms the city into a bustling hub of cultural activities, featuring everything from street performances to open-air concerts. Musicians from various genres grace the stages, providing a soundtrack to the beautiful summer nights. The highlight of the festival is the spectacular fireworks display over the lake, illuminating the night sky and drawing crowds to the waterfront for a memorable evening. It's a time when the community comes together to celebrate the arts, and everyone is welcome to join in the fun.

Fall brings the **Harvest Festival**, a beloved tradition that pays homage to the region's agricultural heritage. Vineyards across Lake Constance open their doors for tours and tastings, inviting guests to experience the fruits of the harvest firsthand. This festival is all about celebrating the bounty of the land, and visitors can enjoy freshly pressed apple cider, local wines, and hearty seasonal dishes made from locally sourced ingredients. Live folk music fills the air as families and friends gather to dance, share stories, and give thanks for the year's harvest.

In winter, the region transforms into a winter wonderland, with the **Christmas Markets** lighting up towns like Meersburg and Lindau. These markets are magical experiences, with twinkling lights, festive decorations, and the enticing aroma of spiced mulled wine wafting through the air. Stalls overflow with handcrafted gifts, delicious pastries, and traditional German holiday treats. Visitors can wander through the markets, sipping on warm drinks and enjoying the cozy atmosphere, while children delight in the cheerful holiday spirit. It's a time for reflection, connection, and embracing the warmth of community amidst the cold winter air.

Throughout the year, Lake Constance hosts numerous cultural events that celebrate the arts, history, and traditions of the region. From theater performances to art exhibitions, each event offers a glimpse into the local culture and allows visitors to engage with the community in meaningful ways. The annual **Bodensee Music Festival**, for example, showcases the talents of both local and international artists, drawing music lovers from near and far. Each concert becomes a celebration of sound and emotion, set against the backdrop of the stunning lakeside scenery.

Attending these cultural events and festivals is more than just an entertainment experience; it's an opportunity to connect with the people and stories that define Lake Constance. Each festival invites you to become part of the community, to share in the laughter, the traditions, and the joy of celebration. Whether you're dancing under the stars at a summer festival or sipping warm cider at a harvest celebration, the memories created in these moments will resonate long after your visit.

Lake Constance isn't just a destination; it's a

vibrant tapestry of culture waiting to be explored and experienced.

8.1 ANNUAL FESTIVALS

Lake Constance is a region that truly knows how to celebrate, with a calendar filled to the brim with annual festivals that reflect the area's rich culture and community spirit. Each festival brings its own unique charm, attracting locals and tourists alike to participate in the joy and festivities that characterize this beautiful lakeside destination.

One of the most anticipated events is the **Lake Constance Spring Fair**, typically held in late April. This festival marks the arrival of spring and is a vibrant celebration of local crafts, food, and culture. The fair features stalls from local artisans showcasing handmade goods, from pottery to textiles, while local farmers present their freshest produce. The atmosphere is festive, with live music and family-friendly activities, making it an excellent opportunity to mingle with locals and learn about the region's artisanal traditions.

As summer approaches, the **Lake Constance Festival** takes center stage in July, celebrating the arts with a variety of performances throughout Konstanz. This festival features a rich lineup of musicians, dancers, and street performers who fill the city with their talents. The highlight is undoubtedly the spectacular fireworks display over the lake, which lights up the night sky in a dazzling array of colors, attracting crowds to the waterfront for an unforgettable evening. The festival is a true testament to the community's appreciation for the arts and creativity.

In September, the **Harvest Festival** welcomes the autumn season with open arms, showcasing the agricultural bounty of the Lake Constance region. Vineyards, orchards, and local farms come together to celebrate the year's harvest with tastings of fresh produce, wines, and traditional dishes. Visitors can participate in grape-picking tours, sample local cheeses, and enjoy hearty meals made from seasonal ingredients. Live folk music adds to the festive atmosphere, encouraging everyone to join in the dancing and celebrations.

As winter descends, the **Christmas Markets** light up towns like Meersburg and Lindau, typically starting in late November and running through December. These markets transform the towns into enchanting winter wonderlands, filled with twinkling lights and the aroma of roasted chestnuts and mulled wine. Visitors can browse stalls selling handmade gifts, ornaments, and delicious holiday treats while enjoying festive performances from local choirs and musicians.

The markets are a perfect way to soak up the

holiday spirit and connect with the local community.

Each of these annual festivals not only provides entertainment but also fosters a sense of community among residents and visitors. They are opportunities to experience the local culture firsthand, making it easy to form connections with the people and traditions that define Lake Constance.

8.2 MUSIC, ART, AND FILM EVENTS

In addition to the vibrant annual festivals, Lake Constance is a thriving hub for ongoing cultural events that celebrate music, art, and film throughout the year. The region boasts a dynamic arts scene, with venues and festivals that cater to a variety of tastes and interests.

One of the key highlights is the **Bodensee Music Festival**, an annual celebration that draws together a mix of local and international artists to perform in various settings around the lake. This festival typically takes place in late summer, offering an eclectic range of performances, from classical concerts to contemporary music acts. The venues range from historic churches to open-air stages by the lakeshore, creating an intimate atmosphere where music lovers can enjoy captivating performances while taking in the stunning surroundings.

Art enthusiasts will also find plenty to love in Lake Constance, particularly during the **Art Fair in Lindau** held in July. This event showcases the works of local and regional artists, featuring paintings, sculptures, and installations that reflect the unique artistic spirit of the area. The fair not only provides a platform for artists to exhibit their creations but also encourages visitors to engage with art through workshops, discussions, and guided tours. It's a fantastic way to immerse yourself in the local art scene and perhaps even discover your next favorite artist.

For film lovers, the **Lake Constance International Film Festival** is a must-attend event. Typically held in the autumn, this festival showcases independent films from around the world, with a particular focus on regional stories. Screenings take place in various locations, including charming cinemas and outdoor venues. This festival is an excellent opportunity to discover new filmmakers and engage in discussions about cinema with fellow film enthusiasts.

Throughout the year, many towns around Lake Constance host smaller cultural events, such as open-mic nights, theater performances, and art exhibitions, making it easy to find something happening nearby. Local galleries and theaters often feature rotating exhibitions and performances, showcasing the creativity and talent of the community.

Engaging with the music, art, and film events around Lake Constance offers a unique insight into the region's culture and the people who inhabit it. Whether you're swaying to the rhythm of a live band, admiring beautiful artworks, or enjoying a thought-provoking film, these cultural experiences create lasting memories and deepen your connection to this extraordinary place.

So, pack your calendar and prepare to explore the rich cultural landscape of Lake Constance; there's always something happening, waiting for you to discover it.

CHAPTER 9

SHOPPING AND SOUVENIRS

Exploring Lake Constance is a journey filled with picturesque landscapes, historic charm, and lively culture, and part of capturing these memories is through the treasures you can bring back home. Shopping around the lake is more than just an errand; it's an experience that lets you take a piece of this unique region with you. From handmade crafts and local wines to regional delicacies and one-of-a-kind gifts, there's something here for everyone. Whether you're looking to indulge in local flavors, explore artisan markets, or find a meaningful keepsake, Lake Constance offers plenty of ways to make your visit unforgettable.

Imagine strolling through the cobbled streets of Lindau or Konstanz, surrounded by cozy boutiques, family-owned shops, and vibrant marketplaces, each one inviting you in to explore its distinct offerings. Shopping here feels intimate, a world away from the large commercial stores found in bustling city centers.

The focus is on quality, craftsmanship, and local

pride. The items you find are often made by skilled artisans who pour their heart into their creations, ensuring that whatever you bring home carries a bit of Lake Constance's charm and spirit.

One of the most popular items to look for is **Bodensee wine**, a renowned regional product that embodies the unique climate and geography of the area. Local wineries along the lake produce exquisite white and red wines that you can take home, each bottle a delicious reminder of your time spent by these serene waters. Some shops even offer personalized labels or mini bottles, perfect for gifting or savoring yourself. Alongside wines, you'll find local spirits and specialty jams, such as elderberry or plum, capturing the flavors of the region in each bite.

For those seeking something truly unique, **handcrafted goods** are a must. Lake Constance is home to a vibrant artisan community that produces everything from handmade jewelry and pottery to wood carvings and textiles. Many of these artisans use traditional techniques passed down through generations, giving each piece a timeless feel. You might come across delicately crafted ceramic dishes, soft woolen scarves dyed in natural colors, or wooden toys and ornaments that reflect the region's natural beauty. These items make wonderful gifts, showcasing the local culture and craftsmanship.

Marketplaces around Lake Constance are brimming with fresh produce, baked goods, and gourmet products that highlight the area's rich culinary scene. Farmers' markets are a great place to sample local cheeses, cured meats, and artisanal breads, each flavor telling a story of the land. You'll also find stalls filled with vibrant fruits, fresh herbs, and fragrant spices, tempting you to pack a little taste of Lake Constance into your suitcase.

Seasonal markets, like the Christmas markets, are especially enchanting, filled with handmade ornaments, wreaths, and holiday treats that create a magical shopping experience.

Shopping at Lake Constance is also about immersing yourself in the stories behind each item. It's not unusual to strike up a conversation with a shopkeeper who can tell you about the history of their store or the origins of a particular item. These connections make your purchases more than just souvenirs; they become memories of the people and moments that made your trip special.

Lake Constance offers a variety of shopping experiences, from bustling markets to quiet boutiques and traditional craft stores. So, whether you're a collector of art, a foodie, or someone simply looking to find a keepsake from your travels, this chapter will guide you through the best spots to find those treasures. Take a little piece of Lake Constance with you to cherish for years to come, and let these items remind you of the beauty and warmth of this extraordinary destination.

9.1 LOCAL CRAFTS AND PRODUCTS

At Lake Constance, the charm of shopping lies in discovering the craftsmanship and heart of local artisans who pour their creativity and tradition into every piece they create. Souvenir shopping here is about finding treasures that capture the region's spirit—handmade items that tell the story of Lake Constance, from its serene landscapes to its centuries-old customs. Among the must-have souvenirs are **Bodensee wines and spirits**. The lake's temperate climate and fertile soil make for exceptional wines, especially refreshing whites like Müller-Thurgau and Pinot Gris, which reflect the crisp, mineral notes of the region. For a more potent memento, try a bottle of Schnapps crafted from locally grown fruits like apples or cherries. These make not only delightful additions to your home collection but are also great for sharing a piece of your journey with friends.

Another gem to bring home is **artisan pottery**. Many workshops around the lake, especially in places like Meersburg, offer hand-thrown ceramics, from delicate plates and bowls to robust mugs painted in earth tones that reflect the natural beauty surrounding the lake. Each piece feels uniquely crafted, often featuring nature-inspired designs like floral motifs or lake-themed patterns, making them perfect for daily use or as decorative items that evoke memories of your time by the water.

For a cozy touch, look for **handwoven textiles and knitwear**. You'll find soft, woolen scarves, blankets, and sweaters made from locally sourced wool, ideal for bundling up on chilly evenings and remembering the lake's breezy shores. Many of these items are made by local knitters who use traditional techniques, infusing each piece with warmth and craftsmanship.

Additionally, wood carvings, such as toys and home decor pieces, are popular. These items often showcase Lake Constance's landscapes, animals, or iconic sights, with each piece exuding a rustic charm that speaks to the region's deep-rooted connection to nature.

And for a sweet and unique souvenir, try **local jams and honey**. These preserves capture the flavors of the lake's countryside, with varieties such as elderberry, plum, and apple. A jar of local honey from Lake Constance's wildflower meadows is an exceptional treat, embodying the lake's natural essence and perfect for spreading on bread or adding to tea as a taste of your travels.

9.2 BEST SHOPPING AREAS

Exploring Lake Constance's shopping areas offers a blend of vibrant markets, charming boutiques, and cozy gift shops, each offering unique finds. Konstanz, as one of the lake's largest towns, is a fantastic starting point. Its **historic Old Town** is full of boutique shops and specialty stores where you can browse everything from artisan pottery and vintage books to handmade jewelry. Strolling through its cobbled streets, you'll find shops that have been family-owned for generations, where each item carries a personal story. Don't miss the

Münsterplatz market square, where local artisans gather weekly to sell handcrafted goods and regional specialties.

For a taste of local flavors, head to the **Ravensburg Farmers' Market**. This bustling marketplace is known for its fresh produce, cheese, meats, and baked goods. Here, you can buy artisanal breads, regional cheeses, and other culinary delights perfect for a picnic by the lake or as delicious gifts to share with loved ones back home. The farmers' market is also ideal for mingling with locals, learning about regional recipes, and experiencing the genuine hospitality of the lake's community.

In Lindau, the **Maximilianstraße** is a shopper's

delight, lined with boutiques that sell everything from chic clothing to unique home decor items. This is the place to find high-quality local crafts and stylish souvenirs. Many shops here focus on eco-friendly and locally sourced products, making it a great area to find sustainable keepsakes. During the holiday season, Lindau transforms into a magical Christmas market, offering handmade ornaments, festive treats, and gifts that capture the warmth and joy of the season.

Meersburg, with its medieval atmosphere, is another gem for shoppers. Its winding streets are filled with cozy gift shops and art galleries showcasing local talent. A highlight is the **Meersburg Castle shop**, where you can buy items inspired by the castle's history—perfect for those looking to take home a piece of Lake Constance's storied past.

Nearby, the Meersburg wine shops offer tasting options and guided recommendations, allowing you to bring home the ideal bottle as a memory of your lakeside experience.

Lake Constance's markets, boutiques, and gift shops invite you to slow down and savor the shopping experience, each area bringing its own unique flavor to the table. From the bustling market squares to the serene boutique-lined streets, there's a shopping destination for every taste around Lake Constance, ensuring you leave with treasures that tell the story of your journey.

CHAPTER 10 ACCOMMODATION OPTIONS

Lake Constance offers a range of accommodations that suit every type of traveler, from those looking to indulge in luxury to visitors seeking budget-friendly comfort. Finding the perfect place to stay can shape your experience, transforming your trip from a simple getaway into a truly memorable escape. The area around Lake Constance—shared by Germany, Austria, and Switzerland—reflects a unique blend of cultures, and this cultural fusion is beautifully mirrored in the hospitality offerings around the lake. Each region and town offers distinct charm and character, providing choices that appeal to both the nature-lover and the culture-seeker.

Imagine waking up to the gentle sounds of lake water brushing against the shore, the crisp morning air filled with the scent of pine and fresh mountain breeze. **Luxury resorts and wellness hotels** around Lake Constance capture this peaceful setting perfectly, combining high-end comfort with breathtaking views. Places like Konstanz and Lindau boast waterfront hotels where you can experience the beauty of the lake right from your room. These hotels often feature wellness spas, heated pools, and gourmet dining options, allowing guests to immerse themselves in total relaxation. For a more intimate, boutique experience, several lakeside inns offer charming, personalized service and beautifully decorated rooms that make you feel like part of the family. These boutique hotels often provide a glimpse into the local history and traditions, with staff eager to share insider tips about the area.

If you're looking for a more budget-friendly stay, **guesthouses and family-run B&Bs** (bed and breakfasts) around the lake offer warmth and comfort at a more affordable price. These options, often nestled in quiet towns or quaint villages, allow travelers to enjoy a cozy setting that feels worlds away from typical city hustle. Staying at a guesthouse in Meersburg, for example, allows you to experience the medieval charm of the town, with the added pleasure of meeting hosts who treat you to delicious homemade breakfasts, local stories, and a warm atmosphere. These accommodations are perfect for those who want to connect with local culture and savor the simple joys of lakeside living.

For nature enthusiasts, **camping and eco-friendly lodges** provide an unforgettable way to experience Lake Constance's natural beauty up close. Numerous campgrounds are dotted around the lake, with options for pitching a tent or staying in a charming wooden cabin. Camping is an excellent choice for those looking to spend their days immersed in outdoor activities like hiking, swimming, and biking, and their nights stargazing by the lakeshore. Many of these campgrounds cater to families, providing amenities such as playgrounds, communal BBQ areas, and activity programs for children.

Eco-lodges around the lake are also growing in popularity, with eco-conscious travelers able to enjoy sustainable, comfortable stays that harmonize with the natural surroundings.

Vacation rentals, from charming lakeside cottages to modern apartments, provide flexibility and a home-like feel, making them ideal for longer stays. Renting a home gives you the freedom to cook your own meals, live at your own pace, and fully immerse yourself in the lakeside lifestyle. Lake Constance's vacation rentals range from rustic wooden chalets to sleek, contemporary apartments overlooking the water, so you can tailor your stay to your own style and preferences. Plus, staying in a rental offers the opportunity to experience life like a local, visiting nearby markets, cooking with regional ingredients, and discovering neighborhood spots that might otherwise go unnoticed.

No matter where you choose to stay around Lake Constance, each accommodation option offers a unique way to connect with the lake and its diverse surroundings. Whether you're unwinding at a luxury resort, savoring breakfast at a charming B&B, sleeping under the stars at a campground, or making a vacation rental your own, Lake Constance ensures a memorable stay that makes you feel at home by the water. Each type of accommodation brings its own special touch to your journey, allowing you to create the ideal experience—one that aligns with your desires and enhances the natural beauty and cultural richness of Lake Constance.

10.1 HOTELS AND RESORTS

Lake Constance is home to a range of hotels and resorts that cater to every style and budget, making it easy for travelers to find the perfect place to stay. For those seeking luxury, Lake Constance offers an array of high-end resorts that blend modern elegance with breathtaking views of the lake and surrounding landscapes.

Imagine waking up to floor-to-ceiling windows that frame the serene waters, enjoying an indulgent breakfast on a private balcony, or unwinding in a spa with panoramic lake views. Many luxury hotels in this region, particularly in places like Konstanz and Lindau, feature not only stunning rooms but also wellness centers, gourmet restaurants, and heated pools. These properties are often nestled in idyllic spots along the lake, making them ideal for travelers looking to relax in a peaceful, picturesque setting.

For a mid-range option, the region offers numerous boutique hotels and family-run inns that provide comfort, character, and a warm, personal touch. In towns like Meersburg and Bregenz, you can find charming hotels that blend modern amenities with classic European charm.

Many of these places are located in historic buildings, allowing you to experience the ambiance of a centuries-old inn while enjoying updated comforts. These boutique hotels often offer exceptional service, with local staff who are more than happy to share insider tips, recommend nearby attractions, and help you feel truly at home in the region.

For budget-conscious travelers, Lake Constance has no shortage of affordable yet comfortable options. Smaller towns around the lake have budget-friendly hotels that still deliver a cozy and welcoming stay. These places may not offer the luxuries of high-end resorts, but they often come with friendly service, clean rooms, and convenient locations close to the lake or public transportation. Budget hotels around Lake Constance allow travelers to enjoy the region's beauty and charm without breaking the bank, making it possible for everyone to experience this magical destination. No matter where you choose to stay, the hotels and resorts around Lake Constance provide a welcoming home base to explore the wonders of the lake and beyond.

10.2 ALTERNATIVE ACCOMMODATIONS

For those seeking a unique and authentic experience, Lake Constance offers a range of alternative accommodations that immerse you in the region's natural beauty and local culture. Staying at a bed and breakfast (B&B) is one of the most charming ways to experience Lake Constance. Many B&Bs are family-run and located in traditional, rustic homes, often with lush gardens and cozy interiors. Here, you can start your day with a homemade breakfast featuring fresh local ingredients, and you'll often find that the hosts are eager to share local stories and hidden gems. B&Bs provide a warm and personal atmosphere that makes it easy to feel like you're part of the community, making them an ideal choice for travelers who value connection and authenticity.

Camping around Lake Constance is a fantastic option for nature lovers, families, and anyone looking to disconnect from the hustle of everyday life. The region has numerous well-maintained camping sites, many of which are located right on the water's edge, giving you a front-row seat to the lake's stunning sunrises and sunsets. Camping here is an immersive experience; you can spend your days hiking, swimming, or fishing, and your evenings around a campfire under the stars. The campgrounds around Lake Constance cater to various needs, from simple tent sites to cozy wooden cabins for a more comfortable stay. Some even have family-friendly amenities like playgrounds and activity centers, making camping a memorable and affordable way to enjoy the natural wonders of the area.

For a longer stay or a home-like setting, vacation rentals offer flexibility, space, and the freedom to settle in at your own pace. Around Lake Constance, vacation rentals range from quaint cottages and lakeside chalets to modern apartments with all the conveniences of home. Staying in a rental gives you the opportunity to explore the region like a local—shopping at markets, cooking with regional ingredients, and enjoying the privacy and comfort of your own space. Vacation rentals are perfect for families, groups, or anyone who values a bit more room to spread out. They often provide an excellent base for day trips around the lake, and many come with outdoor spaces where you can enjoy al fresco meals with lake views.

With options ranging from B&Bs with a personal touch to adventurous camping and flexible vacation rentals, Lake Constance offers something for everyone. Each type of alternative accommodation has its own charm and benefits, ensuring that visitors can find the perfect place to match their travel style and immerse themselves in the beauty of the lake region.

CHAPTER 11 SUSTAINABLE TOURISM PRACTICES

Lake Constance is not just a place of stunning natural beauty and cultural richness; it's also an ecosystem that requires mindful preservation. As more travelers discover the magic of this lake and its surroundings, sustainable tourism practices have become essential to ensure that future generations can continue to enjoy its charm and vibrancy. In this chapter, we'll explore the ways in which Lake Constance and its communities are championing sustainable tourism, making it possible for visitors to experience the region responsibly and respectfully.

Sustainable tourism is more than just a trend here; it's a commitment to preserving the lake's pristine environment, supporting local communities, and honoring the cultural heritage that makes Lake Constance unique. The focus on sustainable practices around the lake encourages travelers to take an active role in conservation efforts.

Whether it's staying at eco-friendly hotels, dining at restaurants that source ingredients locally, or supporting artisans who craft traditional products, visitors have countless ways to make a positive impact simply through the choices they make.

One of the primary goals of sustainable tourism at Lake Constance is environmental conservation. The lake and its shores are home to a rich diversity of plants and animals, some of which are unique to this region. By adopting eco-friendly practices, local businesses and visitors help protect the lake's water quality and surrounding habitats. Hotels are implementing measures like renewable energy use, waste reduction, and water conservation. Many outdoor tour operators are also involved, promoting activities like biking, walking, and kayaking over motorized alternatives to minimize pollution and noise disturbance.

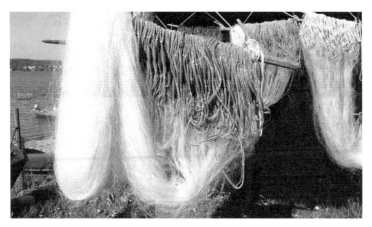

Visitors also find that sustainability at Lake Constance extends to cultural and economic support for local communities. Farmers' markets, family-owned inns, and craft shops provide opportunities for travelers to directly support the region's economy while enjoying authentic local products and experiences. Buying local not only reduces carbon emissions from transportation but also helps small businesses thrive and keeps cultural traditions alive. By choosing to shop, eat, and stay local, visitors contribute to the economic and social sustainability of the region.

Another pillar of Lake Constance's sustainable tourism efforts is education. Guided tours, information centers, and educational programs emphasize the importance of protecting the lake's environment. Many hiking trails, nature parks, and cultural sites offer insights into sustainable practices and conservation efforts, allowing travelers to learn more about how they can minimize their impact while exploring the region. Educational initiatives also encourage visitors to approach their trip with an understanding and respect for the natural and cultural heritage of Lake Constance, which ultimately leads to a more meaningful and responsible travel experience.

Sustainable tourism at Lake Constance is a win-win for travelers and the region alike.

Visitors can experience the beauty and diversity of the lake in an authentic, responsible way, knowing that their choices support the preservation of this extraordinary destination. From eco-conscious accommodations and low-impact outdoor activities to local dining and meaningful cultural interactions, Lake Constance offers a truly enriching experience for those who choose to travel mindfully. This chapter will guide you through the sustainable practices embraced around the lake, helping you enjoy an unforgettable visit that respects and supports the natural and cultural treasures of Lake Constance.

11.1 ECO-FRIENDLY TRAVEL TIPS

Traveling responsibly at Lake Constance goes beyond simply appreciating its beauty; it's about taking small yet impactful steps to preserve the lake's natural environment. Eco-friendly travel around the lake not only benefits the ecosystem but also enhances your experience, allowing you to connect with the region in a meaningful way. Here's how you can enjoy Lake Constance while leaving a positive footprint.

One of the simplest yet most impactful choices is to reduce car usage. With a wide range of well-marked biking trails, walking paths, and public transport options, you can explore the area's stunning landscapes without contributing to traffic congestion or air pollution. Renting a bicycle to tour the lake's perimeter offers a leisurely, scenic way to take in the beauty of the area, all while minimizing emissions. Many towns around Lake Constance offer bike rentals, and there are numerous picturesque cycling routes along the shoreline, through forests, and past charming villages. For those who prefer walking, several trails meander through vineyards, wooded areas, and lakeside paths, allowing for a quiet, immersive experience in nature.

Another eco-friendly travel tip is to pack a reusable water bottle and snacks in reusable containers. Tap water around Lake Constance is often clean and drinkable, so refilling your bottle helps reduce the waste associated with single-use plastics. Similarly, supporting local markets and buying fresh, local produce not only enriches your meals with regional flavors but also cuts down on packaging and transportation emissions. If you're staying in an area that permits picnics, packing a zero-waste lunch can be both enjoyable and sustainable.

Choosing accommodations that prioritize sustainability is also a powerful way to support eco-friendly tourism. Many hotels and guesthouses around the lake are committed to reducing their environmental footprint by using renewable energy, conserving water, and managing waste responsibly. Staying at eco-conscious lodgings helps reinforce the importance of sustainable practices to local businesses and encourages further positive change.

Being mindful of your impact on the local ecosystem is essential, too. Lake Constance is home to diverse flora and fauna, and by staying on designated paths and respecting wildlife, you help protect the natural balance of the area. When swimming or boating, use reef-safe, biodegradable sunscreen, as certain chemicals in regular sunscreens can harm aquatic life. Practicing these simple, eco-friendly habits ensures that Lake Constance remains a pristine destination for generations to come.

11.2 LOCAL CONSERVATION EFFORTS

Lake Constance's commitment to conservation and sustainability is not just a philosophy but a way of life deeply ingrained in local communities. Regional initiatives have transformed the lake into a model of environmental stewardship, where protecting natural resources is as important as promoting tourism. Understanding these efforts can deepen your appreciation of the area and inspire you to actively support them during your visit.

One of the most significant conservation initiatives at Lake Constance focuses on water quality. Local authorities, environmental organizations, and citizen groups have joined forces to monitor and protect the lake's waters, ensuring they remain clean and safe for both humans and wildlife. Regulations are in place to limit pollution from agricultural runoff, wastewater, and other sources, keeping the lake's ecosystem in balance. You can often learn more about these efforts by visiting local environmental centers, which offer informative exhibits and resources for travelers interested in sustainable practices.

Efforts to preserve biodiversity are also a top priority. Lake Constance is home to unique species of fish, birds, and plants, some of which are endangered. Organizations like NABU (Nature and Biodiversity Conservation Union) actively work to protect habitats around the lake, focusing on everything from wetland conservation to bird protection. These initiatives ensure that the lake's natural beauty and biodiversity remain intact, and some conservation areas offer guided tours to educate visitors on the importance of preserving these delicate ecosystems.

In addition to direct conservation efforts, Lake Constance supports renewable energy projects that align with the region's environmental goals. Local governments and businesses invest in solar, wind, and hydroelectric power, reducing reliance on fossil fuels. Several visitor centers around the lake provide insights into these projects, showcasing how Lake Constance is leading the way in sustainable energy for the future.

One of the most engaging ways to support local conservation is by participating in community-led cleanup events. Local groups organize regular shoreline cleanups to remove litter from the lake's banks, and visitors are often encouraged to join. These events provide a hands-on way to contribute to the lake's well-being, meet like-minded people, and feel part of the region's commitment to sustainability.

By understanding and supporting these local conservation efforts, travelers can become part of Lake Constance's ongoing journey toward sustainability. These initiatives are a testament to the region's dedication to protecting its natural resources, and as a visitor, you have the chance to make a positive impact simply by respecting and embracing the area's values. Whether by taking a guided eco-tour, supporting local renewable projects, or simply being mindful of your actions, you contribute to a collective mission to preserve Lake Constance for all who cherish its unique beauty.

CHAPTER 12

PRACTICAL TRAVEL TIPS AND SAFETY

Planning a trip to Lake Constance can be one of the most exciting and rewarding experiences, but to make the most of it, a bit of preparation goes a long way. "Practical Travel Tips and Safety" serves as your essential guide to navigating the lake region with confidence and ease, equipping you with useful, straightforward advice that will help ensure a seamless journey.

In this chapter, you'll find an array of practical information to make your visit as smooth and enjoyable as possible. From packing tips to communication insights, local customs to health and safety pointers, we'll walk you through the essential details you need. Traveling to a new place is about more than just seeing the sights; it's also about feeling prepared, understanding the local rhythms, and making informed choices to enjoy a worry-free adventure. These tips will empower you to make the most of your stay around Lake Constance, giving you the confidence to explore without hesitation.

Lake Constance is a popular destination, but its charm lies in its unique blend of countries, cultures, and experiences. With the lake touching Germany, Austria, and Switzerland, it's a place that brings together a fascinating mix of languages, currencies, and etiquette. Knowing a few basic phrases in German, as well as the local customs, will go a long way in creating positive interactions. Though English is widely spoken, a friendly "Guten Tag" (good day) or "Danke" (thank you) is always appreciated. We'll also cover practical travel tips like understanding the Euro and Swiss Franc, local transit options, and advice on when to visit busy versus quieter spots around the lake.

Safety, of course, is a top priority. While Lake Constance is generally a very safe destination, it's always wise to know what to expect. This chapter includes an overview of local emergency contacts, tips for safe swimming and hiking, and advice on handling the occasional unexpected scenario, like sudden weather changes.

With its vast array of outdoor activities, from water sports to mountain trails, knowing how to stay safe while enjoying all the region has to offer will enhance your experience.

Finally, traveling sustainably is becoming increasingly important, and this chapter will guide you on how to minimize your impact on the environment during your stay. Small actions like using refillable water bottles, respecting wildlife, and sticking to designated paths not only protect the local ecosystem but also help maintain the natural beauty of Lake Constance for future visitors.

With these practical tips, you'll be ready to immerse yourself fully in the magic of Lake Constance, experiencing the lake with ease, safety, and a greater sense of connection to its unique culture and landscapes. Prepare to embark on an unforgettable journey, equipped with all the essential knowledge to make it memorable and meaningful.

12.1 HEALTH AND SAFETY TIPS

Ensuring you have a safe and healthy trip is key to making the most of your experience around Lake Constance. This section on health and safety tips will give you peace of mind by covering all the essentials so you can focus on exploring rather than worrying.

Emergency Contacts: The tri-country region around Lake Constance (Germany, Austria, and Switzerland) is well-equipped with emergency services, but it's essential to have local emergency numbers on hand. For medical emergencies, police assistance, or fire services, dialing **112** works across all three countries, providing you with a single, unified emergency contact. It's also wise to familiarize yourself with specific services in each area; for instance, in Germany, you can dial **110** for the police. Many hotels and tourist centers around the lake also have first-aid kits and can direct you to nearby clinics or hospitals if needed.

Local Healthcare: Healthcare standards are exceptionally high around Lake Constance. Each of the three bordering countries offers top-notch medical facilities, and English-speaking doctors are often available in larger towns, particularly in tourist areas. If you're traveling from within the European Union, an EHIC (European Health Insurance Card) will cover most medical services, though having additional travel insurance is strongly recommended for broader coverage. For non-EU travelers, private insurance ensures easy access to medical services, including check-ups, treatments, and prescriptions if needed.

Safety Advice: Although Lake Constance is known for its friendly, welcoming atmosphere, taking a few basic precautions will enhance your trip. Outdoor activities are a highlight of the region, but always follow safety guidelines when hiking, biking, or engaging in water sports. Be mindful of sudden changes in weather, as the lake can experience quick shifts in temperature and wind, especially in the afternoons.

When hiking or biking in forested or mountainous areas, stick to marked trails, wear sturdy footwear, and carry a map or GPS device to avoid getting lost.

Finally, Lake Constance's water is inviting for a swim, but take note of designated swimming areas and avoid venturing too far from shore, as currents can be stronger than they appear. For boat rentals or paddleboarding, check local regulations and always wear life jackets for added safety. With these simple health and safety tips, you can feel well-prepared and confident as you navigate your adventure around the lake.

12.2 ESSENTIAL PACKING LIST

Packing wisely for Lake Constance can significantly enhance your experience, allowing you to enjoy every activity without feeling unprepared. From seasonal clothing to handy accessories, here's a comprehensive packing list to make your journey as comfortable as possible.

Clothing: Lake Constance's climate varies with the seasons, so packing according to the time of year is essential. For summer visits, lightweight clothing, sun hats, and breathable fabrics will keep you comfortable on warm, sunny days. Don't forget a swimsuit for lakeside lounging and swimming! If you're visiting in spring or fall, layerable clothing is ideal for adjusting to fluctuating temperatures. For winter trips, especially if you plan on venturing to nearby ski areas, pack warm jackets, gloves, scarves, and waterproof boots. Regardless of the season, bring a sturdy pair of walking shoes, as many of Lake Constance's best sights are best enjoyed on foot.

Outdoor Essentials: Given the abundance of outdoor activities, packing for adventure is a must. Include a refillable water bottle, sunscreen, sunglasses, and a small first-aid kit for any minor scrapes or blisters along the way. A daypack is useful for carrying your essentials, whether hiking, biking, or exploring the quaint towns around the lake. If you're an avid photographer, a camera (or a smartphone with a high-quality camera) is a great asset for capturing Lake Constance's scenic beauty.

Travel and Navigation Tools: Lake Constance spans three countries, so it's helpful to carry a compact guidebook or map of the area. A power bank is a lifesaver, keeping your devices charged for maps, photos, and calls throughout the day. If you plan to explore by bike, some bike rental shops provide maps with popular routes; alternatively, downloading offline maps on your phone ensures you stay on track without relying on data.

Local Currency and Essentials: Since Lake Constance touches Germany, Austria, and Switzerland, you may encounter both the Euro and Swiss Francs. Although credit cards are widely accepted, it's advisable to have some cash on hand, especially for small markets or in rural areas. Lastly, a few key phrases in German can be useful, particularly in smaller towns where English might be less common—though locals are often friendly and eager to help regardless of language.

With this essential packing list, you'll be well-prepared for any situation that comes your way, ready to explore, relax, and enjoy all the comforts and wonders of Lake Constance.

Happy packing, and enjoy your unforgettable journey!

CONCLUDING NOTE

As we draw the curtain on this exploration of Lake Constance, it's important to reflect on the myriad experiences and unforgettable memories that await you in this breathtaking region. Nestled at the intersection of Germany, Austria, and Switzerland, Lake Constance is more than just a picturesque body of water; it is a vibrant tapestry woven from rich history, diverse cultures, and stunning natural beauty. Each chapter of this book has aimed to guide you through the many facets of the lake, from its charming towns and thrilling outdoor activities to its delightful culinary scene and thriving cultural events.

Traveling to Lake Constance is an invitation to immerse yourself in a unique blend of adventure and relaxation. Whether you're wandering the cobbled streets of historic towns like Konstanz and Meersburg, indulging in locally crafted wines and cheeses, or exploring the serene waters through boating and swimming, each moment spent here fosters a deep connection to the landscape and the people who call it home. The warmth of the locals, the charm of the villages, and the tranquility of the lake create an atmosphere that beckons travelers to not only visit but to truly experience life at its most serene.

As you prepare for your journey, remember that sustainable tourism practices can ensure that this enchanting region remains vibrant for future generations. By respecting local customs, supporting local businesses, and engaging in eco-friendly practices, you contribute to the preservation of the natural and cultural heritage that makes Lake Constance so special. The more we embrace responsible travel, the more we enrich our own experiences and those of others.

This book has been crafted to serve as your companion and guide, offering insights that inspire curiosity and foster a deeper understanding of what makes Lake Constance an exceptional destination. We hope it encourages you to venture out, explore, and connect with the landscapes, flavors, and stories of this remarkable region.

In closing, may your journey to Lake Constance be filled with joy, discovery, and moments that resonate long after you return home. Let the beauty of the lake and its surroundings awaken your spirit of adventure and remind you of the simple pleasures that life has to offer. Safe travels, and may your experiences around Lake Constance be as boundless as the waters that cradle it.

Made in United States
Troutdale, OR
12/20/2024

27077008R00115